BUILDING WINNERS

*Essential Strategies for
Raising Strong Kids*

Michael Landas

Printed in the U.S.A.

Published By: Ocean View Publishing, LLC

Building Winners

Essential Strategies for Raising Strong Kids
Parenting, Self-Help

ISBN-10: 0-9989928-9-5

ISBN-13: 978-0-9989928-9-1

DISCLAIMER

The purpose of this book is to educate and entertain. The author, guest authors, and publisher does not guarantee that anyone following the techniques, suggestions, ideas and strategies will become successful. The author and publisher shall have neither, liability nor responsibility to anyone with respect to any loss or damage caused, or alleged to be caused, directly or indirectly by the information contained in this book.

Guest authors are in no way connected to Michael Landas or Ocean View Publishing, LLC.

Contents

Chapter 1

It All Begins With You

Let's start with you!

Do you realise that as a parent you are in a leadership role? In business you can define leadership as the ability to motivate, and persuade others to take the actions you want them to take that are in their best interest and the best interest of the business.

As a leader in business you would make things happen that normally wouldn't happen without your presence. In my martial arts school business, I've been responsible for changing the lives of many kids because I was able to convince them and their parents that my service was right for them. In most cases, the amount of convincing involved was minimal. It was more like putting it in the proper perspective so they could make a decision that was in their child's best interest.

They all thanked me for helping them years down the road. In humanitarian leadership (the leadership I most admire), leaders are responsible for causing millions of people to support a cause, give help in some way, or change their feelings on a particular subject. Think of greats like Dr. Martin Luther King or Mother Theresa, or a less than positive example Hitler. These leaders used their power of speech and their belief in their cause to persuade others to action.

Some of these examples apply to family and some don't. However, if you take the time to study leadership as a way to enhance your parenting skills, you will see what I mean. But let us now move on to what I believe to be the number one law of leadership as it applies to parenting.

Lead by example, both of you. Your children will follow your example of how you live your life up until the point they are able to decide for themselves. And at that point they'll still look to you for leadership in some way.

But you'd have to agree with me that if they have a good example to follow all those years when they still think you're "number one," they'll be much better off. Everything we do as parents should be with the intention of making our kids upwardly mobile. We want to contribute to enhancing the next generation. In other words, we should want our kids to make more of a contribution to society than we ever did.

Here's an example: If I write three books in my life and consider it a way of leaving my mark, that's fine. On the other hand, if my daughter wants to become an author, I would hope for her to either write more books or sell more than I ever did. If she doesn't want to write a book, that's fine too. To make our children unstoppable, we can't set any limits on their potential. Regardless of what our level of contribution and service to others will be in our lifetime, we should hope that our children out-perform us in all that they do—as long as they achieve happiness and success in the process.

We learn from our experiences, that's common sense! One definition of common sense is to have an experience, good or bad, and then draw lessons and knowledge

that we can apply to subsequent experiences. This ties in perfectly to parenthood because we've got twenty, thirty, and sometimes even more years of life's experiences than our children. We bear the responsibility to steer our children clear of any regrets or mistakes that we've made. It's just common sense that each generation doesn't make the same mistakes!

Begin to embrace your leadership role and use every chance you get to inspire your child to achieve great things!

Chapter 2

The Keys To Raising Your Child For Success

Since this book is a guide for early-to-late childhood, the idea is that we will be as proactive as possible. Raising our children on a rock solid foundation—a foundation of self-esteem and confidence, family values, pride, and a desire to do what brings value to others and satisfies their needs to make accomplishments.

Many of the seemingly minor issues that affect our children can be suppressed by giving them one important character quality, self-esteem! Self-esteem is the degree to which your child feels himself to be a worthwhile, important person. Many psychologists feel, and I do as well, that self-esteem in children has its roots in unconditional love. You know you love your child! You take it for granted that they understand you love them. But loving them alone is not enough to build their self-esteem. You need to be careful about all types of communication that you have with them, good and bad.

Have clear rules based on correct principles of right and wrong—values for the family.

Point out that they are in violation of the rules, which will be obvious since you've already established them clearly.

Don't yell! Yelling brings out anger and it's hard to communicate with love if you're angry! Easier said than done right? But answer this question: Have you ever felt good after verbally bashing your children or spouse? Chances are you said no. When you yell you beat up on your own self-esteem as well, and remember as the leader you must set the standard and be an example at all times. This is the responsibility we have, and it cannot be taken lightly.

Don't violate your own principles—Hypocrisy would be the term here-To say something and do another. Hypocrisy among parents can take many forms so we're not going to get into a lengthy discussion of obvious hypocritical behavior. Instead, we'll discuss seemingly small ways you can be hypocritical and the long term affects that it can have.

Little Lies—Leaders, genuine leaders don't compromise on principle. What happens when you take the kids to a buffet for a family night out? Let's just pretend that one of your children has recently become a teen. Now they are considered by buffet standards to be an adult, and no longer qualify for the child rate. You, in a moment of quick decision, say two adults and two children please. Your son, who is recently thrilled about becoming a teenager (we know you're not happy about it, but you'll adjust) and wants to be treated like an adult, looks at you as if to say "I'm not a kid anymore." You pick up on the look and quickly give him a look of your own, as to say "I just paid a stupid parking ticket today, if I can save a couple of bucks on dinner I'm entitled.

So you get the kids' price and during dinner your son asks you why you said he was a kid. Now, the worst thing you can say is "Oh that's right you just had a birthday" as to try to cover it up. You don't go that far, but you tell your son, "Well you just turned thirteen and I paid this ticket that I didn't deserve, so I figured what the heck, why not save on dinner?"

What's the mistake you made? This is a relatively simple example. In essence, what you taught your thirteen-year-old son is that it is ok to lie so long as you have a good reason. This lesson now sticks with him, and when he lies to you about what seems to him like a small matter, you'll know where it came from. What you just did was give him an example of how it's fine to lie as long as you can justify it. And if you can recall what leadership rule number one was: Lead by example!

The phone rings and you're busy, your seven-year-old daughter picks up the phone. She says: "Mum it's for you" and you say, "tell 'em I'm not home." What's wrong with this picture? The problem may seem insignificant at first. A little white lie is not a big deal you may think, but when you get your child involved it is a big deal, greater than you can imagine.

When that phone rings and you instruct your child to tell the caller you're not home, when in fact you're sitting right there, you're allowing your child to lie for you. And when your child lies for you, you're teaching them that it's ok to lie to you! You'd be much better off instructing your child to inform the caller that you are indeed busy and cannot take the call, and the caller can try again at a specific time. When you do this, you'll teach your child courtesy and honesty. Two virtues that we do our best to instill at CFTA Martial Arts.

Never compromise on principles when it comes to your child. The long-term damage is never worth the immediate gratification. As Emerson said, "guard your integrity as if it was a sacred thing." Guard your family values and principles as they were a sacred thing, because they are.

Chapter 3

Parent Leaders Are Good Communicators

A valuable skill of parenting is the ability to get information out of our children—information that you can use to understand them better while helping them with problems and challenges. There are many problems that you've already had and have learned from, why have your children go through the same pain?

In our rapidly changing world, times are certainly different and occasionally you may find yourself saying, "I never had to deal with this when I was a kid." Although the technical portion of the problem may be different, the root causes basically remain the same over the years.

Kids' problems usually manifest themselves in social situations – i.e. not getting along with another child. Problems in school. Problems that arise during sports and activities. The list goes on.

The greater their self-esteem and confidence, the less time you'll spend on these issues. How you deal with these issues and the communication lines you establish between you and your child will minimize the big issues that could come up during the teenage years.

Self-esteem is the degree to which your child feels himself to be a worthwhile person. At CFTA Martial Arts in Coffs Harbour, Australia, we teach martial arts lessons to kids and families all over Coffs Harbour. Our passion is to make each student feels special through the goals they accomplish!

Chapter 4

Always Be Ready To Talk To Your Child

Children are on a different wavelength than us, their brains and emotions function in the moment. We can't expect them to always plan the time that they want to open up to us on any particular topic. If they're ready to communicate, it is our obligation to drop what we are doing and hear them out. I know, this may seemed far-fetched, but remember it takes too much work to get them to the point where they are even willing to open up, we can't throw it away because we are watching Australian Idol!

At times this will be tough. Imagine it is April 14th, and you are doing your taxes (which I don't recommend unless you're an accountant) and your child needs to communicate with you about what they feel is an important topic. You'd be wise to give them a certain number of minutes and try to resolve the issue and if you cannot do it within the time you have allocated, explain to them the situation and pick up the conversation the next day. The point here is that how many times are you really doing something that is so worthy of your attention that it warrants more attention than your most precious possession? Leaders are good communicators and are always ready to help their followers.

It is through your ability to ask questions and persuade that you gently lead your child in the right direction. When they reach out for your leadership most, you have to be ready to give it to them!

At CFTA Martial Arts, children learn about leadership as they advance in rank. In martial arts, colored belts are used to signify experience and mastery of techniques. The children are taught that moving up in rank automatically puts them into a leadership role. The children with lesser experience and knowledge look up to them because they're working towards that particular rank. Since every child in CFTA is a leader, they must learn and understand the first and most important rule of leadership: Lead by example.

If we can be great examples for our children to follow by setting high standards for ourselves, being good communicators, reading and learning constantly, and being ready to listen, our children will follow us instead of the local gang. They will respect us for walking our talk and will adhere to the values that we lay down as a family. In the process they will become winners. As a parent, remember this line—If you set the example, you won't have to set the rules.

Leading by example is the most important leadership lesson that a parent can apply. When you boil down this principle of leading by example, you will discover that your actions are the most important form of influence you will have over your child. It will not be what you say, or say you're going to do. It will only be what you take action on and follow through with. That is what leaders do—they take action.

We thought being decisive was enough, but just making a decision doesn't necessarily do anything. I'm reminded of a tale about three birds that were sitting on a branch. Two birds decided to fly away, how many are left? You might say one after you do your simple math. The fact is unless I say two birds "flew" away, how many are left you can't answer. The fact is we all *decide* to do things, but less people take action on their decisions!

Your actions are not simply a function of what to get started on either. Your actions are how you carry yourself all day, how you treat others, and how you take care of yourself. "What you do, mum and dad, speaks so loudly, I, as your child can barely hear what you to say." And when it comes to your action remember…

"A picture is worth a thousand words, but an action is worth 1000 pictures, so an action is worth a million words."

I first heard this great saying from Martial Arts Grand Master Jhoone Rhee. Grand Master Jhoone Rhee is known as the father of Taekwondo. Throughout his career, he has taught taekwondo to countless celebrities and government officials. He is a true leader in the martial arts world and has inspired many of us to follow our dreams and teach martial arts professionally.

Chapter 5

Teach Your Child How To Set Goals
Leaders set goals based on clear visions!

If you are a parent you have goals for your child. They may be growth and developmental goals, academic goals, and maturity goals. As parents we want the best for our children. Now we must teach our children how to want the best for themselves by teaching them how to set goals!

Teaching your child how to set goals will be fun for the whole family! In fact after you help your child set their goals you can begin clearly setting your own, which will have a huge impact on you reaching them faster.

Here's how to start. First, define a goal. I like to use this definition: A goal is a planned destination, a desired result. Or in kids' language; "A goal is something that you want." Goals help us stay on track. They give us reasons to do our very best. Once your child understands what goals are, they can begin to set goals in three areas: Academic, maturity, and athletic.

It is effective for a child to set yearly goals and review them each month to measure how far they've come. What if they don't reach their goal? Extend the deadline, that's all.

Let's get back to setting them. On a clean sheet of paper have your child write the three categories at the top. Then under each category they will write as many goals as they can think of. Here's one example "I graduated the fourth grade with honours, June, 20__." This would be an example of an academic goal. Notice that we put the goal in the first person, present tense, and we state the goal as if it were already complete. It's very important that you follow this procedure, by doing so your child's goal will become part of their subconscious mind. Make sure your child re-writes their goals monthly. You can begin your own list of goals and review them monthly as well.

By having your child do this exercise each month you will be doing them a huge favour! It will take discipline on your part, but if you can follow through and stay with it you will give your child an edge.

In our Martial Arts program we use Black Belt as a long-term goal that each child will set for themselves. By setting this goal children learn the importance of tenacity and follow through in any activity. I want to end this chapter with our "Black Belt Success Cycle:" Know what you want, have a plan and a success coach, write it down, take consistent action, review your progress and renew your goals.

Chapter 6

How to Develop Self-Discipline

Self-Discipline is the master skill of leadership and success.

What is self-discipline? Self-discipline has been defined as the ability to make yourself do what you know you should do, when you should do it, whether you feel like it or not! A disciplined person knows what has to be done and does it. They don't put it off until later or allow themselves to be easily taken off track. And, most importantly they prioritize and focus on being self-disciplined with activities that move them toward their goals. There's a big difference between having self-discipline with tasks that don't move you toward your goals and doing very well what needs not be done at all. It's usually the more challenging activities and tasks that will help you reach your goals than those of less importance. This concept is easily confused, so be careful which activities you exercise your self-discipline with.

When teaching children self-discipline, it is important to have fun and keep in mind that the idea is to establish routines that are followed for the entire week without deviation or distraction. We want our children to pick up after themselves, to clean their rooms without being told, to study and do their homework on their own, and to be responsible for their extra-curricular programs as well. We demand a whole lot from them!

Explain to them that there are two kinds of discipline: Parent discipline—we constantly tell them what they need to do! And self-discipline—they take care of certain things without reminders from us! Sometimes, just understanding this simple concept can point them in the right direction!

List all of their responsibilities that have to do with, school, home, extra-curricular, and leisure time. Have a discussion about all their responsibilities in those areas. Then, with their input, teach them how to prioritize. In other words make sure they know that homework and studying are more important than chores. Remember the self-disciplined person does the more important goal-oriented activity first.

When your child understands what's important by the goals you've have set it will be easy to establish a comfortable routine for everyone to follow. Your routine should include all the activities on your list. The more regimented you child becomes and the more you and him plan time for every responsibility in order of importance, the more discipline he will have. Just remember to stick to a fun routine so it becomes habit, and therefore causes your child to want to be self-disciplined.

Chapter 7

What Are We Thinking?

Leaders think positive thoughts.

We all think in pictures. Many times what we see in our mind translates to what we end up with in reality. The great challenge lies in being able to control what kind of pictures that play in the theater of our mind! This month's lesson is important and practical for both parents and children,

What kind of thoughts do you habitually think? What kind of thoughts does your child habitually think? Although we would like to believe our thoughts are of success, accomplishment, and a bright future, they may not always be. If we took an inventory of our thoughts we might discover from this audit that we dwell on past failures, present problems, and future anxiety too much. No matter how good you or your child's current situation, we can all benefit from tighter control of our own thoughts.

Why is this so important? Many of the psychological breakthroughs of the last century had to do with the fact that "we become what we think about most of the time." Just that one sentence should awake you to how important this topic is to you and your child's future success. This is mainly due to the power of the subconscious mind, which processes every thought and experience we have. The subconscious actually doesn't know the difference between a real event and one that is vividly imagined. I encourage you to do your own research on the subconscious mind to further your study!

Your assignment is to catch yourself thinking thoughts of fear and failure, and then to quickly change them to positive successful thoughts. Just being aware of your thoughts and this fact will have a huge impact on your success.

The best way to help teach your child to control his thoughts is with a fun concept called visualization. Positive visualization or mental rehearsal, as it's sometimes referred to, is practiced by top performing men and women in all kinds of situations. Athletes, entertainers, public speakers are just a few of the professions where the champions rely heavily on this discipline. We have a theater in our mind and it's open twenty-four hours a day! Positive visualization is how we make sure that good movies are playing. So how can this help you and your child?

Let's pretend your child has an important project that will require him to speak in front of his class or maybe the entire school. Now keep in mind this is just an example, but the idea is to use visualization on just about everything, especially the tasks which he may feel challenged and fearful of. Say to him something like this. "Son it's your turn. You feel calm, your muscles are relaxed, you're breathing easily, you're on your way up to the stage and you're taking your time. You stand confident and speak clearly. Everyone can't wait to hear your presentation. During your presentation, everyone is focused on you because you are doing such a great job. You finish and everyone claps! You did fantastic!"

Using the theater of the mind to rehearse success will be very powerful for you and your child. I encourage you to try it! Just remember when you visualize and self-talk, (Incidentally, Zig Ziglar says, it is okay to talk to yourself. It's even fine to answer, just as long as you don't say "huh?" to the answers) you have to imagine vividly that it is actually happening. You must also talk and visualize in positive terms, "I am relaxed", "I gave a great presentation." And not "I will not screw up."

Chapter 8

The Listening Posture

"Focus your eyes, focus your mind, and focus your body!"

Parents: Have you ever found yourself wishing that your son or daughter listened better? Do you feel that just a slight improvement in their listening skills would make a huge difference in their potential?

Getting your child to absorb 100% of what you're telling them is a challenge that many parents and teachers face. Did you ever wonder, "Boy I hope he listens in school better than he does at home?"

If your son or daughter could improve their listening comprehension just 10% it would have a profound impact on them don't you agree? So here's what you can do…

First understand that your child is forced to deal with dozens of external distractions duringthe course of the day: TV, radio, classmates, computers, and the list goes on. These external distractions, combined with your child's internal distractions, (the inability to control one's thought process) causes most listening problems.

Make your child aware of these two distractions, internal and external. Teach him the difference between each, and then get him to give you examples of when each one affected his ability to listen. Just this knowledge will make him a better listener.

Teach your child the importance of focusing his eyes, ears, mind, and body. Focusing all four will engage him totally in the listening process. Make sure your child knows that when it comes time to listening, the first thing he has to do is look into the eyes of the person talking.

When his eyes are focused he could then tune in his ears to the message and process it in his mind. Now you're getting somewhere!

Finally, teach him about standing or sitting up straight when listening. If the body is out of focus or slouched, the message will not be clearly understood.

Maybe you could hold off on delivering your message until his body is focused and upright.

Becoming aware of these simple but effective concepts will go a long way toward helping your child be a more focused listener. Try them out and see how they work!

Chapter 9

How to Overcome Social Anxiety

Maybe it has happened to you before. Your daughter is scheduled for her first dance lesson, karate class, or soccer game and you get her to the class or the field and she freezes! She just doesn't want to get into the class or step on to the field! Your son's first baseball game is Saturday and he's been talking about it all week. "I can't wait to hit the ball, I can't wait to run the bases, I can't wait", he says. Then, when the time comes to get his baseball uniform on and he refuses! Or how about when you feel as though a particular activity will be beneficial for your son or daughter and you say, "Hey would you like to give ___ a try?" and they say "No!" You then ask why and possibly unintentionally argue about how it's no big deal to try things!

In my 20 years as a martial artist, school owner and instructor, I've witnessed my fair share of children who seem to become disinterested at the moment of truth. If this has happened to you, don't worry about it and don't be mad at your child.

All that happened was a slight case of social anxiety brought on by the thought of stepping out of their comfort zone. If you were able to get them there because they were excited and then they suddenly changed their minds all that happened was simple. Their mental picture did not match what they now were seeing in reality. If you asked them about trying something and they said, "No!" Then they simply already made a mental picture of themselves being uncomfortable.

We all have social anxiety. It's not easy to step out of our comfort zones. Just imagine attending a party where you don't know anyone? Or, if you're fine with that, how about speaking in public? The key fact to remember is our kids are no different. But the sooner you help them step out of their comfort zone the easier it will get each time. If you give up the first time the harder it may get!

There is a psychological principle called systematic desensitization, which simply means that the more you make yourself do what you are sensitive or fearful of, the less sensitive and fearful you will be. Thus, if your child experiences some social anxiety, don't let it bother you too much, just keep trying and don't give up, social skills and the ability to control fear are essential in our world and the sooner your child begins developing these skills the better.

In the next few chapters you'll hear from a few of the most popular parenting advice authors in the world. They were all extremely generous with their knowledge and expertise so that you and your family could benefit.

I'll join you to wrap off this book in the last two chapters.

Chapter 10

How to Defeat the Bully

Your child is forced to deal with various attacks on his self-esteem on a regular basis.

Whether these attacks affect him long term or not, has to do with many different factors.

One type of attack is the common "Bully." Bullying has always been a part of growing up, but how a child deals with it and the repercussions of dealing with it have changed dramatically. There are "Zero Tolerance" rules that punish both children if there is an altercation, (which may have been caused by one child bullying the other.) So the old "If they hit you, hit 'em back!" doesn't fly today. Compound this with the fact that most bullying situations take place during non-school hours. So the threat of consequences is non-existent. So what is your child to do?

First of all, we must recognize that incidences of bullying vary in severity. One thing that is certain is that repeated attacks whether verbal, physical, written, or on the internet erode your child's fragile self-esteem. The CDC linked bullying to isolation, drug use, violence, and suicide! But your child does not have to be a victim!

The assault can be verbal or physical, either way, the first line of defence remains the same. Self-Confidence! Here's why. Bullies choose their victims much like a criminal would choose their victim; they go for the easy and obvious target. If your child looks like a kid who will get bullied, guess what, they're going to get bullied. One the other hand, if your child radiates self-confidence they are less likely to be a victim. It's almost that simple!

Your child needs to walk with their head up, their shoulders square, and make eye contact with people. Just doing so, even if your child needs work on their self-esteem, will keep bullies away from them. This is easier said than done, but it can be learned. Having them change their body language (what they say or are saying non-verbally) will have a huge impact. Teaching this can serve as a quick fix, however, going to work on their self-confidence will have a greater long-term effect on keeping bullies away.

Children get their first layer of self-confidence from their parents. The love you show your child and the time you spend with them gives them their feelings of self-worth. It has been said that the number one role of parenting is to develop a self-confident individual.

Teach them how to speak up clearly when they first meet someone, and the importance of eye-contact when they talk to you. Get them out of their comfort zone and have them explore new things. The more you have them confront fear and discomfort the more confident they will become.

Kids learn by doing, and when they begin to accomplish goals that they didn't believe they could, their self-confidence gets a boost. This in turn effects every area of life making them less of a target for bullies.

Chapter 11

Teaching Good Sportsmanship By Hal Runkel

Teaching good sportsmanship to our children is one of the great responsibilities of parenthood. Unfortunately, "good" sportsmanship isn't the only thing they can learn from their coaches, teammates, and you. So, how do we go about teaching this valuable lesson to our kids in a culture that seems to value it less and less? Good question.

I believe there are three elements to sportsmanship: rules, etiquette, and culture. As a coach and as a parent, I try to pay attention to all three.

Rules. Rules are simply the structure of the game itself. Every sport has established rules that provide the freedom to play, much like railroad tracks give the train freedom to travel. The rules of the game are the non-negotiables and the best way to teach those rules is by obeying them ourselves. Cheating, in any way, is not just a bad example, it actually introduces the very chaos and instability of life that sports can help us conquer.

Think about it—life is very confusing and difficult. It is full of ever-changing people playing by ever-changing rules. Sports, at their best, invite us into a small world that can protect us from that chaos by providing a clearly agreed upon structure that encourages freedom of expression and friendly, growth-inducing competition. When parents and coaches fail to teach the rules of the game, and fail to obey those rules themselves, sportsmanship is not the only casualty. Chaos triumphs over stability and security as well. Something for us all to think about when tempted to play our best little league player a few more innings than the time allows, or tempted to secretly send coaching signals to our budding tennis phenom.

Etiquette. Like rules, the practices of a sports' etiquette can differ greatly from sport to sport. But unlike rules, these practices are not enforceable by referees or umpires or league commissioners. The practices of etiquette are not agreed upon by rules committees; they have evolved as a way for sports to retain a spirit of courtesy and respect between combatants and for the game itself.

In tennis, for instance, you shake hands over the net after a match. In baseball, you line up on the baselines and congratulate the other team with your right hands at the end of the game. In boxing, you touch gloves at the beginning of the first and last rounds. In basketball, you volunteer your culpability, after a bad pass, a defensive lapse, or a hard foul. And perhaps no sport has more specific practices of etiquette than golf, from staying quiet during an opponent's swing to avoiding someone's putting line on the green.

These "rules" of etiquette are not published in bylaws somewhere, nor even discussed between opponents before a game, but violating them can arouse as much anger as cheating. Etiquette is what makes the game humane, what elevates the game above animalistic conflict.

What is absolutely important is to focus on how you and yours adhere to these practices much more than on how anyone else does. It's easy, and important, to publicly call out rules infractions committed by anyone involved in the contest. It's equally important to quietly practice the etiquette yourself without telling anyone else they should as well. This is an area where examples speak loudest. So exhibit the best etiquette yourself, teach your child to do the same, and then both of you be quiet about anyone else. When it comes to etiquette, it is far better to be viewed as an example than ignored as a know-it-all.

Culture. This is the area of sportsmanship that is the least clear-cut, but can be the most influential. All sports have a unique culture surrounding them, a culture which silently governs attitudes, shapes coaching and playing styles, and can even influence personalities and relationships outside the playing field. And it is because of this powerful influence that I advise parents and coaches to pay very close attention to it.

Take football, for instance. Football creates and maintains a very unique culture, with both positive and negative applications. On the positive side, football creates a very team-oriented culture. It is perhaps the most team-oriented sport of all because of its relatively rigid position roles and requirements. This team emphasis in football is a remarkable metaphor for all the interdependencies that exist in life.

Another element of football culture that is not so positive, in my opinion, is the emphasis on toughness, or even meanness. Just go to a Pony League practice and watch the wannabe coaches running the elementary kids till they puke and then making them pick it up with their hands (I've seen it happen). No sport carries the "go to war" mentality like football, and that part of football culture is the reason behind the current concussions controversy in the NFL, as well as newly discovered dogfighting craze among NFL athletes. "Toughest is best" is football at its worst.

Thankfully, there are scores of examples of talented, successful football players who demonstrated incredible toughness while also exuding respect for their opponents, their own bodies, and the idea that it is still only a game. Walter Payton comes to mind as an example from my youth; Peyton Manning shines today. These men were able to follow the rules of football competition, practice exemplary etiquette toward other players and the game, and exist as "tough, but respectful" beacons within the football culture.

There are other players in other sports who are able to succeed in their sports without fully succumbing to the worst parts of the culture of those sports. Wayne Gretsky never fought in a hockey game. Jack Nicklaus never cursed on a golf course, and never talked badly about another player. Tim Duncan never talks trash on the basketball court. Roger Federer never loses his cool on the tennis court (but he does host a pizza party for the ball boys & girls at every tournament). Talk about these players with your spouse in front of your kids; root for these type players on TV; invite your kids to admire them with you.

It is our job as parents and coaches to shape the culture of our families and our teams. Ask any business leader how difficult it is to shape the culture of a company—it ain't easy. But the truth is that shaping a culture happens anyway. Every second of every day we function as leaders. How we behave as leaders constantly shapes our surrounding culture, both positively and negatively. How we cheer for our teams, how we talk about other players and opponents, how we speak with the coaches and other parents, whether and how we volunteer for snack duty, how we confront rules violations—all of these are constantly shaping the cultures of our families and our teams. And the kids are not just watching us, they're inhaling the cultural air around them.

There is no magic recipe to follow to make our kids into respectful competitors. I can only offer a viewpoint that helps us remember that how we participate in sports is a character issue, one that can extend far beyond the boundaries of the court. And since, according to our ScreamFree Parenting philosophy, the greatest thing we can do for our kids is focus on ourselves, this is character issue first and foremost about ourselves.

Hal Edward Runkel, MS, MMFT, LMFT, is one of America's leading experts on family relationships. A therapist, relationship coach, seminar speaker, and organizational consultant, Hal is the founder and president of Scream Free Living, Inc., and the author of Scream Free Parenting. Visit: www.screamfree.com

Chapter 12

Staying Positive: Lessons From Life To Help You Succeed
by Charles Seymour Jr

Plant Grass, Stop Pulling Weeds
It's Feedback, Not Failure
Keep Going – The American Idol Way

My daughters often tease me about my **Saving The World, One Soul At A Time.**

I can't say that I'm aiming for the WHOLE world, but one person at a time is a great beginning.

Let me give you a little background: There's a part of our brains called the Reticular Cortex (sure hope I have the correct) and it sees what we tell it to focus on.

As an example, when you purchased a new car, did you notice all of a sudden that there were LOTS of them on the road that you had never noticed?

Or maybe when you were writing a paper for school, out of the blue a very important point came to your mind and an example was on the front page of the newspaper you were reading.

Did those things just "happen" to be there OR, because you were now energetically focused on something, did you just happen to NOTICE them?

The answer is clear: you just happened to notice them.

On my website, RaisingGreatFamilies.com, I decided that I didn't want "negative" material. No negative quotes from world heroes, no matter how profound. No negative jokes by stars of the golden era of TV even though they still make me laugh. No books about the 7 Worst Things Your Kids Will Do Before The Age Of Five.

Just positive energy emanating from the site. Why?

So that the reticular cortex of EVERYONE'S brain could focus on the GOOD in our world, allowing people to see MORE good.

See how that works? We focus on the good and we SEE the good.

The same is true for you, your children, and how we see our children.

How often has your child brought home a report card and most of the grades are really good but one is not. What do YOU focus on...all the great achievement or the one area where he or she fell short?

Believe me, I'm not saying to forget the shortcomings. I'm a positive guy, not naïve. We need to be there to help them in areas that aren't their strongest. But how much better will our children do if we accentuate the positive (as the old song goes) instead of droning on about the negative?

Here are three good stories to amplify this. Plant Grass; Stop Pulling Weeds

There was a young couple who bought their first house. Their dream was to turn it into a loving home with several children. The young husband did everything he could around the house to turn it into a beautiful environment for him and his wife, but he just couldn't get the muddy patch from the front yard to turn into a nice lawn. His wife suggested that her husband call her father who had had beautiful lawns for as long as she could remember. When the father-in-law came over, he instantly saw how to fix the lawn problem. "Keep planting grass. Stop pulling weeds. "For you see, the husband was focusing most of his time on getting rid of the bad (the weeds) and not enough on culturing new good (the new grass to grow).

"Keep planting grass. Stop pulling weeds." And the lawn turned into a showplace that the young family used for years as their playground.

Good advice for all of us.

Keep positive. Banish negative. Keep working with the good and downplay the bad, but use the bad as feedback as to what you are doing.

Keep planting grass, and enjoy your life. It's Feedback, Not Failure

How many times have you set a goal (and its timetable to accomplish it) but fell short of making it? Often, if you set lots of goals, I'm sure. I know that's how it is with me. But I learned a long time ago that I don't "fail." It's just feedback to me:

- I took on too much and couldn't meet the deadline.

- People didn't want what I was offering, so I had to change how I presented it.

- The goals I set may not have been realistic, so I need to rethink them.

Carol Burnett, the TV icon (and VERY funny and insightful woman) says it this way: "You have to go through the falling down in order to learn to walk. It helps to know that you can survive it. That's an education in itself."

Thomas Edison, the great inventor of the light bulb (among other things) could have stopped many times. At least 10,000 times, in fact! But did he consider himself a failure? No Way: "I have not failed. I have just found 10,000 ways that won't work," he said when inventing the first light bulb.

Notice the positive attitude?

Notice how some people get down when others aren't effected at all?

Kahlil Gibran, the artist, poet, and writer, said it this way: "Your living is determined not so much by what happens to you as by the way your mind looks at what happens."

See? Attitude.

Not only is your never-say-stop attitude paramount to your success, so is your setting goals and working toward them.

"The fight is won or lost far away from witnesses – behind the lines, in the gym, and out there on the road, long before I dance in the lights."

Could that apply to you?

And who said that?

- A soldier working to strengthen his body to meet all upcoming challenges?

- A dancer on "Dancing With The Stars" before each week's episode?

- A karate student who understands how important practice and discipline are?

It could have been all of them…but in THIS case it was the greatest fighter ever to live: Muhammad Ali.

So, what do Carol Burnett, Thomas A. Edison, Kahlil Gibran, Muhammad Ali, and YOU have in common?

You all know:

- how to get back up when you are down,

- how to set goals and let nothing get in your way until you succeed

- how to prepare yourself LONG before the results are on the line.

Keep going and never give up…which leads into our third lesson.

American Idol – Stay At It Even If Others Think You Aren't The Best

Did the best person win American Idol in 2009?

Maybe.

Did the best SINGER win? No way.

But remember, American Idol is NOT a singing competition. Forget what Simon Cowell and Randy Jackson say about it being a singing competition— would Sanjaya have EVER MADE it onto the air in 2008 or William Hung seasons earlier?

No way.

The competition in 2009 came down to Adam Lambert vs. Kris Allen: Vocalist vs. Nice Guy.

What would have happened if Kris Allen had listened to all the "experts" who said that Adam was the best?

Adam Lambert can REALLY sing. He has a great instrument. (Hey, I'll put my own track record of singing, directing, CD producing, theater directing on the line and say I can tell a singer in "2 notes" (as they used to say on Name That Tune)). BUT…did all the "raccoon makeup" (as I read somewhere), dark nail polish, nearly Goth-like clothing (at times) scare off his voting public?

Kris Allen is a really nice guy but NOT a great singer (see my credentials above). Close your eyes and just listen to him to see if his voice is what you want to hear on your next CD. NICE guy. Family guy. Has a beautiful wife and a dad who shares his emotions and cries. All makes for GREAT TV.

Simon Cowell was pushing WAY too much for Adam. Others were lavishing praise, but you could almost feel Simon's wallet screaming out to us: "Vote For This Guy to make me even richer." Truth be told, Adam won't need #1—he'll still make it. His name will be remembered MUCH longer than…oh, right, who DID win it last year?

Kris was better at connecting with the public who was voting. Did you notice the scruffy appearance when it was clear he would be put up against Adam? Adam had the black finger nail polish and thick eyeliner makeup. But Kris seized on this, scruffed it up, had video with his mom and dad, showed his wife and child, etc. Played great into the heartland of America.

Did you notice the final judges comments to Kris on Tuesday night of the last week? They were basically saying, "Hey, you're a nice guy, you did your best, you deserve to be on this stage, BUT… And the silent part was: "But you ain't gonna win."

It was the most one-sided, "We Love Adam" display of the entire season. The coronation had taken place…except the American Public hadn't spoken yet. Do you think the public "sensed" this even if they weren't sitting there analyzing it as I was? You betcha.

Did you see Simon's face when Kris was announced the winner? He was dumbstruck. The other judges were smart enough to stand up and applaud the gallant winner but it took Simon until Kris and the rest of the gang were standing on the raised platform behind the judges before Simon acknowledged Kris by standing and shaking his hand.

And the biggest lesson: Somehow Kris spoke to his voting public and gave them what THEY wanted and Adam didn't. Was it Adam's high-note, tongue-showing display of power-singing (making many of his songs sound the same) vs. Kris's piano playing, guitar playing, just stand-there-and-sing style? Was it the nice boy vs. the somewhat scary, hard-to-feel-comfortable-with guy? And who were the voters—teens who will scream for Kris vs. rockers who will scream WITH Adam?

Whatever the reason, Kris resonated with his "customers" and Adam didn't.

But again I ask: What if Kris Allen had listened to all the "experts"? All of them were saying that Adam would win. What if Kris believed in his heart that he had no chance against Adam Lambert and had given up?

He would have lost.

Henry Ford said it pretty well: "If you think you can or you think you can't: you're right."

So take this example and learn from it: Never Give Up. Stay at it no matter what those around you say. Set your goals and stay focused. And teach this to your kids – they watch YOU and learn from YOU even when you don't think they notice.

Be positive and tell yourself that you CAN... and you will. Learn from the lessons all around you and keep going: your best is still ahead of you.

Charlie Seymour Jr is the founder of:

http://RaisingGreatFamilies.com,
http://UltimateWork-AtHomeDads.com, and
http://ILearnedItAllFrom-MyKids.com.

He also helped his younger daughter sell her first music CD through her site: *http:// LizSeymour.com*. Charlie is living life with the 'Oz' Philosophy: Courage, Brains, and Heart. He's a Blogger, Philosopher, and Marketing Evangelist. Helping Ultimate Success Dads achieve their financial best! You can reach him at *LessonsFromLife@ CharlesSeymourJr.com*

Follow Charlie on Twitter:

http://twitter. com/UltimateWAHDads

© 2009 *CharlesSeymourJr.com* and SMO Marketing LLC. All Rights Reserved, though frequently permission is granted for use for e-zines, blogs, radio programs, TV news, and magazines. If you want to use something you find here, please email Use *Permission@UltimateWorkAtHomeDads.com*

Charlie is very supportive of the work of Ocean View Publishing, LLC

Chapter 13

Learning to Listen and Communicate
by Cathi Cohen

All elementary-school-age children need guidance to improve communication skills. Some children require more assistance than others. How do you determine if your child needs extra help developing conversations with peers? The following are some questions you can ask yourself to clarify the issue.

1. Does your child look the person he is speaking to in the eyes?

2. Does your child actively listen when he is spoken to?

3. Does your child allow others a chance to speak and be heard?

4. Does your child speak in a calm, pleasant tone of voice?

5. Does your child show interest in another person by asking questions?

6. Does your child keep his body still when speaking with another person?

7. Does your child initiate conversations with others regularly?

8. Does your child talk on the phone with other children?

9. Are your child's statements and questions in a conversation relevant to the topic at hand?

10. Does your child use appropriate body language with others?

11. When others are talking, does your child make supportive statements such as "that's great!" or "Wow!" or "Yeah!" or "Me too!"?

If you answered each of these questions with a sounding "Yes!" then it sounds like you can skim this chapter. Continue to highlight conversation in your everyday interactions and support your child's ability to empathize appropriately with others.

If you answered some of these questions with "Not really" or "No," you might want to try some of the tips and exercises listed below.

Improve Parent/Child Communication First:

I can't overstate the value of having discussions with your child to help model conversation skills. I recall working with Mrs. Jones, a mom who was quite concerned about her daughter's trouble conversing with friends. She said Ashley appeared distracted and preoccupied when talking with others and continually changed the subject back to herself. Was Mrs. Jones surprised when she realized that she herself struggled to listen to Ashley! She found herself often tuning her daughter out and becoming distracted by household matters. She was pleased to see that when she became a better listener, Ashley followed suit and became a better communicator with her friends.

Make Sure Your Child Knows You Are Listening:

Schedule 15 minutes a day to sit down with your child and "schmooze". Look at your child when he is talking to you.

Ask Open Ended Questions:

Rather than asking a question that requires a "yes" or "no" response like, "Did you have a good day?" try asking questions that help your child

- 59 -expand upon the question. For instance, you might ask like, "Tell me what you did in PE Today." Or, "What is your coach helping you with in basketball?"

Listen Without Judgment:

Avoid reactions like, "Why did you hit that boy on the playground?" Instead try, "Tell me about what happened on the playground today."

Stay Focused and Interested:

Talking about "lunch" or "PE" may seem boring or banal to you, but for your child it might be a time of social interaction that he wants to bounce off of you. Sometimes you learn the most fascinating pieces of information from your child when you least expect it!

Remember Details So That You Can Follow Up:

"So how did your art class go? I know you were working on a clown painting yesterday."

Check In With Family Members at Dinnertime:

Give family members a chance to share a little about their day, and allow others to listen actively and respond enthusiastically.

Use "I" Messages: For instance, "I feel frustrated when you don't listen to my directions the first time." This is a kinder, gentler way of saying, "You never listen to me."

Reinforce Positive Communication Behavior:

When you see your child engaging in good eye contact or active listening, be sure to praise it! For instance, "Boy, Charlie, I feel so good when you look at me when you are talking." "You know, Jen, I really like it when you listen to me when I talk to you."

Make Sure Your Child Is Looking at You When You Talk to Him:

This will help your child develop good eye contact with others. Children have a lot of trouble seeing themselves the way others see them. They need your help recognizing how others see them and how their behavior affects others. Good eye contact is the backbone of good communication.

Remind Your Child Gently To Use His Indoor Voice:

Your child may be unaware of how he sounds to others. You are his monitor and can help him hear himself. You can even reward him for every hour his voice level remains low.

Tips for Helping Children Communicate Better

✓ Use a Code Word to Remind Your Child to Use Good Communication Skills

You might use a word like "EYES!" or "LOOK!" to remind your child to look in the eyes of another person. This code word acts as a prompt without embarrassing your child unnecessarily.

✓ Play the "Freeze: Game

At the dinner table, say, "Freeze" and look to see who is paying attention to the conversation. Praise family members who are following the conversation.

✓ Reward Your Child For Listening

Give him a star or sticker. You can tell if your child is listening because he is:

- looking in the other person's eyes;

- keeping his body still;
- allowing the other person to speak without interruption; making sounds that express interest like "Oh," "Uh huh," "Yeah."
- asking questions when there is a pause;
- making statements when there   is a pause.

✓ Role Play With Your Children

Children love to play act. See how long they can keep a conversation going playing the part of someone else.

✓ Reinforce Your Child's Patience When He Waits Before Speaking

Immediately pay attention to your child when he asks a question following a pause. If you ignore him when he has successfully waited, he may not recognize that he has done something right. On the other hand, ignore your child when he does not wait for the pause.

✓ Tape Your Child In Action

Play it back and let your child hear himself through other's years. He might be surprised at how he sounds.

✓ Use Hoola Hoop

Ask your child to stand in the center of a hoola hoop, or draw a three-foot circle on the ground around him. Let him experience how far away he should be from others when talking to them.

✓ Develop a List of Dos and Do Nots

Review the list periodically, and praise the skills you see your child "do." Here is a sample list you can add to:

✓ Do's

✧ wait for a pause to speak;
✧ ask appropriate questions;
✧ use a clear and pleasant tone of voice;
✧ look others straight in the eyes.

✓ Don't

✧ don't hog the show
✧ don't change the subject to talk about yourself; don't interrupt

✓ Communication Games and Exercises

TV Talk Show Host:

Allow your child to interview you and to be interviewed.

The host of the show has three goals:

- help make your guest feel more comfortable through active listening;

- ask questions of your guest that show interest;

- share information about yourself that relates to your guest's topics.

The guest has three goals:

- answer the host's questions politely;
- stay focused and on topic;
- use active listening skills

✓ A Communication Ledger

Develop a weekly conversation journal, which tracks and reinforces positive interaction. You can reward your child with stickers, points or stars to be traded in for privileges.

✓ The Reflective Listening Game

This is extremely challenging and feels unnatural to play. The point is to exercise your "listening muscles" *not* to actually listen like this in everyday conversation.

Family member A begins a conversation: "How was your day today?"

Family member B must reflect back what A said before: "You want to know how my day was? My teacher yelled at me. How was your day?"

A responds: "You want to know how my day was. And you had a bad day because your teacher yelled at you. I'm sorry you had a bad day. My day was uneventful."

B responds: "Your day was uneventful. Thanks for the sympathy on my day."

✓ What Comes Next

This game will help you and your child deepen conversation. How to play? A family member brings up a topic of conversation. It becomes your child's challenge to think of a question, which relates to the topic that will bring the conversation to deeper levels.

As parents and adults, we recognize the importance of strong communication and conversation skills. It is critical that care and direction be taken during the formative years to develop and reinforce these abilities. Without these in place, development of the more complex social skills is, at best, difficult. Take time and effort to work with your child to give him the tools he needs to grow in a positive direction.

Cathi Cohen is the founder of In Step, a private mental health practice in Fairfax, VA, and Stepping Stones, a social skills group training program for children and their parents. She can be reached at *www. insteppc.com*

Chapter 14

Persuasive Skills for Parents
by Dave Frees

Parenting is a display of leadership. Our children model after us, especially when they are young. Even though more and more people come into their lives as they grow up, initially we are the people that they see most often, they're exposed to most often and that they are really imprinted with how we communicate with one another – how we do our problem-solving, how we make decisions, how we make important judgments. And we are influencing them whether we know it or not.

As a parent, you have to take on all these roles, so great communication skills make you much, much better at all of these other things!

Now I'm going to share with you six words; a six-word question that is called the game changer. Everything changes after this. You may be a little skeptical about this at first, but once you've used this question to handle different situations and are convinced of its results, you will probably go, "Hey, the guy was right about this technique all along!"

Even if it works 5%, 10%, or 15% more often to make you really effective as a communicator or persuader, it will be totally worth your while.

Parents: You will have no problems coming up with more than fifty ways in which this question will be useful to you. So let's get started!

Have you ever tried to get your child to do something, perhaps to go to school, eat something that looks new to him, take a musical class, or maybe it's to go to class and train, and your child says, "No, I can't"?

How would you normally respond to your child in those scenarios? If your answer is, "Yes you can", then you are in unison with most other supportive parents out there. That's what we all say because we want to be supportive and we want to keep it positive.

But here lies the problem.

It violates a fundamental law of persuasion and influence, which is that we've gone right to argumentation. In other words, the kid says, "I can't", and you say, "Yes you can". You are taking the exact opposite position, and good negotiators and great communicators know that you always start, no matter where you're going with this, with the outcome that you want in mind and you find some place of agreement.

So what happens is that we violate that rule when we go, "Yes you can", trying to keep them positive. We are doing what we have been taught to do as good communication, but biologically, we have to look at how the child processes that information. They said, "No I can't", and you say, "Yes you can". This causes them to internalize, "I just told him, I just told her that I

MICHAEL LANDAS

can't!" And they play all the reasons in their mind that they are right and that you are wrong, which is the exact opposite of what you want if you want to be successfully persuasive.

Although we are trying our best to be positive, that is not the best way to go about encouraging and supporting our child. When we say, "Yes you can" we're just arguing with them.

Here is the trick.

We are coming up with the six-word question. Anybody can do what I'm going to reveal to you here, because this isn't something new at all. Nobody has to believe what I'm saying here because I encourage you to test it for yourself.

The next time your child says, "No I can't", you say, "I know you feel like you can't." That is agreeing with them, right? Internally they are going to go, "Hey, mom gets it, dad gets it! I said I can't and they I feel like I can't."

Notice the subtle difference there.

This is all happening subconsciously at lightning speed. Sometimes, this internal dialogue surfaces consciously, but usually it occurs so quickly that they feel agreement from you. Notice that they've moved from "I can't" to "I feel like I can't", which is less permanent.

So they say, "Wow, he agrees with me and I feel like I can't." They have shifted the concept from permanence to impermanence.

You can also use other variations such as, "I know you feel like you can't yet", which is a presupposition yet presupposes that they will be able to at some future point. If not now, then soon. Again, as the child processes that he says, "He's right, I feel like I can't yet." They now have the experience that linguistically and in their body that they will be able to.

Instead of arguing with them, you have already moved them twice from this permanent state of "I can't" to "I feel like can't yet." Two very different sentiments at play here.

And now to make it more emotionally-charged and intriguing, and therefore more persuasive and influential, you say, "Hey, come lean in here for a second," or "Where's your mom?" or whatever— do whatever is necessary to make what you're about to say seem interesting and activate curiosity.

This is where you pop the six-word question: "What would happen if you did?"

There are many of variations on this: "What would happen if you could?", "What would have to change so you could do it easily, right now?" But here's the catch. When I say what would happen if you did, what must they imagine in order to understand my sentence?

That's right—the outcome.

Your children have to imagine themselves being able to do it. It is close to impossible for them to understand the sentence, internally or biologically without first imagining themselves doing it. Then, doing it is a disentail part. I haven't asked them to do it nor told them to. See the difference? I said, "What would happen if you could?"

By the way, this technique works with adults too.

"I don't know, I don't know dad..."

"Well if you did know what would it be?"

"Oh, it would be..."

It is really astonishing and amazing how often that works. And by the way, even if it doesn't work, it is amusing and you have actually changed the relationship from confrontational to intriguing, interesting and amusing and therefore, engaging.

Try it.

The next time you catch yourself going about the old habitual, ineffective way of supporting or encouraging your child, experiment on this simple technique of persuasion and feel the difference immediately!

David Frees is an Ivy League educated attorney, author, and an internationally known speaker on the topics of enhanced persuasion, ethical influence and family and business communications skills. He has written and contributed to four books: The Language of Parenting, Einstein's Business, YOU, Inc., and The Ultimate Success Secret. Dave has appeared on Fox, NPR, and PBS discussing family communications and business and persuasion skills.

Dave can be reached at: *http://www.successtechnologies.com/*

Chapter 15

The Delicate Balance of Self-Esteem
by Tina Nocera

Three high school boys sat in the back of the car. In typical fashion, they believed a chauffeur's glass prevented the driver from hearing their conversation. "I can't believe I didn't make the baseball team," said Billy.

"Well, what did you expect—you suck," said Larry.

"No I don't. I always made the All-Star team when we played in Rec," replied Billy.

"Sure, 'cause your dad was the coach," said Larry.

The third boy, Mark, was silent, raising his eyes to look up at his mom through the rearview mirror. He didn't say a word, but he was sure his mom was recollecting a conversation they had a few years back when Mark once again was not selected for the All-Stars. "But Mom, I'm a better player than the kids picked for the All-Stars, but they were picked because they are all the coaches' kids." "I know, but I suppose it is sort of payback for the dads giving up their time to coach. I am not saying it is right, but it is what it is," his mom replied.

Did Billy's dad really help his son by putting him on the All-Star team? Not a chance. If anything, he actually hurt his son's self-esteem by inflating his abilities and setting expectations that he wouldn't be able to meet in the future.

He would have helped his son much more by spending time with him one-on-one practicing in the park. But when the dad took on the role of coach, he took on a responsibility to teach all the kids the game and treat them fairly. We all know that doesn't happen when parents become overly involved in children's team sports.

Today's parents micro-manage what is supposed to be a great lesson for our kids about teamwork, skill, and putting the right person in the right job. What kids learn is that much like bullying, the bigger kid (in this case the father) wins, at least in the short term. The loser, of course, is his own child in the end, who doesn't understand what happened when his dad is no longer involved.

Every generation of parents wants their children to have better lives. Our hope is that they will be successful, but that is often defined in *our* terms of success, not theirs.

Our generation of parents invented a wonderfully, albeit overused phrase, called self-esteem. We were told that if we didn't arm our children with healthy self-esteem, they wouldn't amount to anything.

Although well intentioned, we've taken the concept of self-esteem and jumped the chasm to superlatives. Our children aren't just smart; they are gifted. They aren't just playing sports; they are the next Tiger Woods, Serena Williams, or Sarah Hughes.

I think we missed the point. Self-esteem is about what a person thinks of him or herself, and it is best developed when a child is loved unconditionally and receives acceptance from his parents.

The Right Kind of Self-Esteem

Is it possible to have too much self-esteem? The same question can be raised about having too much good health. The answer is probably not. At the first sign of any problem, the experts point to low self-esteem under the premise there wasn't enough self-esteem. Perhaps it isn't more self-esteem that is needed, but rather the right self-esteem.

William James, the first American psychologist, created a formula in 1890:

$$\textbf{Self-esteem} = \textbf{Abilities} \div \textbf{Pretensions.}$$

Loosely translated, self-esteem equals your abilities (what you can do) divided by your pretensions (your goals, or basically what you want to do). The better you are at things you want to do, the better your self-esteem. If you want your child to have greater self-esteem, figure out ways your child can do better at the things she loves to do.

In our house, we have a standard phrase, "I'll always love you no matter what you do, but I may not like what you're doing." My children have used that on me at times when I was really angry with them.

They would ask at the obvious height of my anger, "But you still love me, right?" It's amazing that no matter how angry you are, you do still love them.

Self-esteem can be defined as being comfortable in our own skin and knowing that we are loved, as they used to say, "warts and all!"

There has been so much written on the concept of self-esteem it is no surprise that we have all taken it so seriously. Actually, I find it all a bit overwhelming and thought it would be helpful to narrow it down to a few ideas. First and foremost, it all begins with you. You cannot give to your children what you don't have yourself. The behavior we model has an enormous influence on our child's development of self-esteem.

Establishing Rules

Setting and establishing rules and limits is as important to children as keeping a promise. From the time they are three or four, we should explain that being part of a family means participating in ways to make the house function well. By now, they are certainly used to watching you run around cleaning up. They really want to be a part of all that *fun*.

Begin by encouraging them to pick up their own toys and put them away when they are finished. This sets expectations for children and says, "We are a family and we work together – every-one helps." The real value is that we all struggle to spend time with our children while trying to balance the tasks we have to accomplish. By including the children in the tasks (no doubt, with their help, some will take longer), you are with them and can talk to them about what you are doing and why you are doing it.

Set Them Up to Succeed

Giving your child the right tools sets them up for success. Think about a time when you were at your job and you were asked to tackle a project. If no one told you the goals of the project, or if you lacked the right skill set for the project and weren't certain of the deadline, you would feel you'd been setup for failure.

Much of success involves putting the right person in the right job, which could have a domino effect on everything else; when nepotism, favoritism, and political appointments are allowed, we all suffer.

It does not matter if a cat is black or white, so long as it catches mice.

-Deng Xiaoping

Think of experiences you may have had when the wrong person was in a job, whether it was a mechanic, doctor, teacher, or haircutter. What's disturbing about this is that parents could very well play a role in perpetuating this practice.

For example, if a child doesn't belong in an honors class, but the parent insists the child is placed in an honors class, then there are a number of possible outcomes:

- The child will fail because she is in over her head.

- The child cheats to stay in the honors class.

- If a number of parents insist their children are placed in the honors class when they don't belong, the teacher will have to dilute material, which means the children that actually belonged in that class didn't learn honors material. This could result in the true honors students, and the teacher, becoming disillusioned. At that point, we all lose.

Parents who do this are teaching kids that they can't live outside the bubble that's been created to protect them. It's really no different from professional athletes taking steroids because they can't live up to the ever-increasing performance expectations.

What is Real Talent Worth?

A woman was strolling along a street in Paris when she spotted Picasso sketching at a sidewalk café. She asked if he might sketch her and charge accordingly.

Picasso obliged, and in just minutes, there she was, an original Picasso. "And what do I owe you?" she asked. "Five thousand Francs," he answered. "What! It took you only minutes," she politely reminded him. "No," Picasso replied, "it took me all my life."

Let Them Be

From the time our children are very little, we put superlative labels on their activities. If they pick up a baseball bat, we envision them in the major leagues. A little girl attends her first dance class, and she is labeled a prima ballerina.

We need to just let them be. We are putting our emphasis on things that honestly don't matter to our children; half the time they don't even know the names of the superstars we are comparing them to.

A superlative is the best, brightest, prettiest, smartest, fastest, which is how you are judged by others. I don't even know how you could possibly measure who is the best at anything. Lasting self-esteem has nothing to do with what other people think of you because it's something you can't control.

When we use superlative labels on our kids, they have an overly-inflated and false sense of self-esteem. It's called the Lake Wobegon effect, where the women are strong, the men are good-looking, and all of the children are above average. What happens the day your child learns that it isn't true?

Do the Math

There are over six million children that play Little League baseball. The New York Yankees have a 25-man roster. That means .0004% of the kids playing Little League baseball will end up on the Yankees. Here are some other interesting odds:

- You have about a 1 in 2,000,000 chance of being struck by lightning.

- A pregnant woman has a 1 in 705,000 chance of giving birth to quadruplets.

- Someone eating an oyster has a 1 in 12,000 chance of finding a pearl inside of it.

- You have a 1 in 9,366,819 chance of winning the lottery.

The moral of this story is simply let your children learn a sport and enjoy playing it. After all, when they start a game, they say *play ball*.

Conversation Starter – *Ask your children how parents should behave at youth sporting events*.

From *Because Kids Don't Come with Manuals®: Contemporary Advice for Parents* by Tina Nocera. Available on Amazon.com Visit: *http://www.parentalwisdom.com/* a parenting website so unique it is protected by two U.S. Patents.

Chapter 16

Five Keys to Raising A Happy, Healthy and Successful Child
by Terri Khonsari

Every child has the potential to be a success. There are different levels of athletic ability, financial advantage, educational availability and a host of other factors, but the fact remains that attitude is what makes a child a success or a failure—and anyone can have a good attitude. This is the one thing that levels the playing field, allowing any child in the world to succeed. A good attitude can be fostered by parents who demonstrate one themselves!

Parents who want their children to succeed will model a good example for them and follow simple steps to ensuring their child learns accountability for his or her own life. If a strong foundation is built from early youth, these children will grow to be responsible, inspired leaders and can carry

these qualities with them into adulthood. Happy, healthy and successful children grow into happy, healthy and successful adults!

Even busy parents have enormous opportunities to be a force for good in their child's life. The way children see their parents behave is what will determine their subsequent attitudes towards life. If children see their parents exhibiting perseverance and responsibility, emphasizing the importance of education and healthy habits, and role modeling good behavior and attitudes, they too will strive for the same level of perfection.

Perseverance

The earliest lesson a child can learn is not to give up. This starts in early infancy, as a baby learning to walk is cheered on and encouraged to try again after falling over. It continues on through early childhood, as they learn to eat by themselves, toilet train and tie their own shoes.

As a child reaches school age, the responsible parent will stay involved, encouraging them to persevere as they struggle to complete homework assignments, or to qualify for a sports team. If they are taught to never be satisfied with giving anything less than their best, they will become adults who are known for excellence in all that they do. You train your child to play their own game of life at the highest level and be the best they can be! And always remember the best your child can be is not necessarily the best you think they should!

Role Models

Parents who think ahead will be sure to introduce their children to role models who can be admired and looked up to for more than athletic prowess or vocal ability. Sports heroes and rock stars can be admired for their natural talent and showmanship, but role models that exhibit deeper traits are needed even more. Historical figures make great examples of men and women who had human failings yet exhibited many stellar qualities worthy of emulation.

Mothers and fathers should remember they are their child's first and best role models. What is said and done by parents is always examined closely and imitated. Caring parents will strive to set examples worthy of their children, and not make the mistake of falling back on *'do as I say, not as I do.*

When a mistake is made, admitting it and moving forward will gain a child's respect more than trying to blow it off.

Responsibility

Responsibility is another trait learned at a parent's knee. When children are shown how to take on responsibility, make commitments and keep promises, they are learning skills that will help them in the years ahead. Responsibility has to be ingrained in all areas of their lives, from taking charge of their own health and education to learning how take a personal interest in their own success in the world.

Children should also be taught the value of money from an early age. A smart parent will show their child how a budget works and explain financial concepts as they become old enough to understand. This can be done by giving them the opportunity to earn and teaching them the importance of saving, spending wisely, and giving to others.

Education

Education is such an important part of the modern world that it cannot be ignored. Sheer academic aptitude is not the goal, but eagerness to learn and diligence at schoolwork and studying new things can earn children powerful tools to use in the years ahead. Parents should show that they too are still learning and that it is a lifelong process by taking every advantage presented to expand their own knowledge.

Travel is another way of contributing to the education of a well-rounded child, and gives them an appreciation of different languages, cultures, and customs. This can be of great value later in life, enabling them to be at ease when mingling with people of varied background and ethnicity. There are many opportunities which every parent can take advantage of to go abroad or bring the world into their home. These include participating in a student exchange program, taking children along on business trips, or skipping vacation for a few years to save for a trip abroad.

Healthy Habits

Health is the final gift a parent can give their child. It is simple to teach good hygiene and eating habits when they are young if good food choices are presented and the value of keeping a healthy body is explained. Parents can motivate their children by teaching them the reasons for including healthy foods in their diet (greater energy and endurance for sports, feeling good and energized in their daily lives). Then the child will keep making healthy choices when they start to make their own selections outside the home.

Mental, emotional, and spiritual health are as important as physical health. It doesn't matter how much money or material possessions a family has. The simple things are the ones that really count, and caring, involved parents can show their children the meaning of happiness just by spending time with them doing spontaneous things. Quality time wins out over quantity time, every time! Teaching children to find the joy in everyday life is a gift that lasts forever.

A child raised up by a parent who believes that they can be something truly spectacular will live up to that belief. When parents take an active role in their child's life, leading by example and teaching them the importance of perseverance, good role models, responsibility, education and healthy habits, children can become superstars. All children have this potential. It is the responsibility of the parent to nurture it. These are the key ingredients to raising a happy, healthy and successful child.

Terri Khonsari is the Author of the best- seller: *Raising a Superstar: Simple Strategies to Bring out the Brilliance of Every Child*

Chapter 17

The Winner's Profile— To Ensure Yours, Your Families and Your Child's Success

If you put several successful families, parents, and kids together and studied them, you surely find some major differences. Differences in culture, certain values, religious and political beliefs and a few others are just par for the course in a free world. However, among the many differences you'd find several commonalities. The commonalities make up the "winner's profile."

Ambitious—Ambition is the want for more, and not being satisfied with the way things are. Ambition causes us to cultivate the desire for greater success in whatever we do—raising our children, managing our family, taking on a new career or business, or working for charitable causes. Ambition makes us want to do our very best, and it teaches our children the habit of striving for more.

Ambition motivates us toward constant, which is the key discipline for getting ahead in the information age. Ambition is good for everyone when used to achieve goals that don't violate the laws of nature or the rights of others.

Honesty—The winner is honest with himself, and that makes it possible to be honest with others. Never forget the letters WIIFM. This is most people's favourite radio station and it stands for "What's In It For Me". Be very honest with others about your motives for doing something. People appreciate the honesty and it'll get you much further along. A good example is when my martial arts school does fundraiser programs for local causes. The way it works is parents pay for a brief martial arts program, we teach the classes, and the charity keeps 100% of the money generated. I am very upfront and direct when I tell the charitable cause that this is a great way to raise some money, but it also gives us a chance to showcase our program with the direct result being many of the students enrolling in our program after the fundraiser is over. It just wouldn't be true if, when the people asked why I did these fundraisers and I responded, "Because I'm a nice guy." That's true but it doesn't tell the whole truth, and remember a winner is completely honest. After I tell them about the program they can easily see how everyone comes out a winner!

When it comes to honesty, many people get into trouble because what they said they were going to do or promised, didn't quite match up to what actually unfolded. Many of us have been on both sides of that dilemma. However, we can decrease this problem for all if we simply live by the saying, "under promise and over deliver" or "go the extra mile". Never forget to under promise and over deliver!

Be honest with yourself when it comes to goals and expectations. Honesty helps the goal setting process tremendously because it forces you to hang in there and pursue rather than to say, "Well, at least I aimed high!" By setting honest goals for yourself and teaching your children to do the same, you will systematically achieve more of your goals over time. This honest success will lead to greater successes and more ambitious goals.

As you can see, our discussion on honesty is a whole lot more than simply telling the truth. I feel, and you'll probably agree, that the truth is always the way to go. What I will teach my child martial arts students about honesty is simple; "If you plan to lie, plan to lie for your entire life." Being honest is not something that you do most of the time, it's something you do all of the time. Of course, there are some very small exceptions. A fellow school owner once told me this story at a convention: "Yesterday evening a parent approached me and asked me for a couple of minutes of my time. I invited him into my office and we began talking about the sudden suicide death of his son's grandfather. The father was not close to the grandfather at all since he and the boy's mother have not been together for years. His son still saw his grandfather on a regular basis. We discussed many details of how we would break the news to his son. We both learned a great deal from the conversation. One of the key points we agreed on was the "suicide" part would be left out for now! We felt that too much honesty in this case would not have been good for his seven year old son." So there are some exceptions. I believe that honesty is always the best policy.

Integrity—As honesty is to your external actions, integrity deals more with you on the inside. Integrity is simply living truthful to your values and what you know in your heart of hearts is right. Integrity is best displayed by someone who acts true to their dominating and guiding principles and doesn't bend or twist them. Lack of integrity can be seen when someone compromises a core value for temporary pleasure or short-term gain. In many cases, the immediate gratification is short-lived and the individual is looking for another quick fix or fast money not too long after. Integrity is doing what you know and believe is the right thing to do. There is no second guessing or questioning yourself when you act with integrity. Acting with integrity makes winning decisions easy.

Congruency—Congruency is similar to integrity because it again is about keeping words, intentions, values and actions in a straight line. You can realize congruency in your life in many ways.

One easy example is doing what you love to do as a career. If you are doing exactly what you love to do, then the line between work and play is very blurred. Living your life exactly as your mission and goals state is the ultimate form of congruency. Many of us are striving to reach this point. The key is not to become stuck in our current situations. The way to discover what you really want out of life is to ask yourself this question: "What kind of skills and talents do I possess that can be most effectively marketed and turned into financial security and freedom?" The reality is that just "doing what you love" may sometimes not be enough to get you the rewards required to live well in our society.

What kind of life do you want to lead? When I asked myself that question the answer came back: "Martial Arts can help me impact the future and do what I love!" So answer the question for yourself and you'll begin moving toward a life of congruency, or perhaps discover that you're already there.

How we use congruency at CFTA —Everything we teach is congruent to our philosophies about what it means to reach black belt (the ultimate goal). Therefore, we always teach in a manner congruent to achieving the principles of "black belt excellence". They are honesty in the heart, have knowledge in the mind, and strength in the body. Establish a set of family, parenting, and personal values that you can be congruent on.

Children and congruency—How can we get our kids to be congruent? Teach them values like, honesty, integrity, and smart work. As they begin to discover themselves, encourage them to follow their interests and develop talents in those areas.

Generate their interest in play, not work. When your child begins viewing martial arts class or your Sunday catches as "work," it can be all downhill from there if you are not careful. So keep everything fun and playful. Remember good martial arts teachers and good coaches will work with you to keep your child on track and engaged in their activities!

To develop their talents and skills in certain areas, you need mega-congruency as I have stated earlier in so many ways. It's better to guide your child to success in any activity than to push them. If you lay down goals of commitment and values ahead of time, you will be acting in total congruency when the time comes to re-motivate them with a sport or activity. Do remember that letting your child give up at the first sign of difficulty, real or imagined, is incongruent to success and will have a lasting negative effect on them!

How I explain it to students is quite simple. Many young students express an interest and desire for achieving Black Belt. This is a very healthy long-term goal. The problem arises when their parents don't believe that they can do it. Here's what happens. A child tells his mother and father that he wants to get his black belt someday. The parents respond with "That's great, but first you have to start practicing more and being more dedicated to your training. I don't want to have to remind you every time we go to martial arts class."

What's happening here is that their parents do not believe that their child's actions are congruent with what they see as the picture of black belt. Parents see our black belt students around the school and they see confident, dedicated, respectful, mature boys and girls. I've met some parents over the years who want the results even before the achievement of the goal. They want the dedicated student or the confident mature individual three years before we can deliver that result to them. Just like it takes some time for a garden to grow-it takes some time to grow an excellent black belt.

I understand how parents feel. At the same time, I also know that setting a goal for your child that they want and are enthusiastic about is something you do for them, and not to them. I know it can be frustrating when kids want to give up on something.

I just pull the student aside and say this, "You say you want to get your black belt and that you want to be in master club." They respond with a nod. "But what's happening here with is you are acting incongruently with what your parents expect from a child who wants to reach black belt. You're telling them that you want it, but what you are showing them is a student who doesn't feel like practicing when he should be. Or you are not behaving in school how a black belt would behave." Whatever the case may be, the child usually begins to understand what I mean. They understand that congruency is matching up what you say with what you do.

Discipline—We've discussed discipline before. So we know that it is a key characteristic of a winner. Discipline is your ability to carry out the plans you have made in order to help you reach your goals. Discipline is making the time and finding the time to do the kind of activities that lead to productive outcomes. We all have the same twenty-four hours in day—a winner makes the best of his time.

We must show our children the discipline we have by making the most of our time. We can show our children discipline by taking steps in the directions of our goals. We can teach our children self-discipline by showing them how to be productive on their own without us always having to tell them. But more importantly, we can give them the quality of doing the important things that need to be done on their way to achievement. We can teach them how to value their time. They'll able to use this self-discipline to make accomplishments as children and adults.

Winners plan to win, prepare to win, and expect to win. Winners hold themselves in high esteem by truly believing that they deserve better. They believe that they are worth more. (Not compared to anyone else but to themselves.) Winners expect the best because they have taken the steps to ensure that the best happens. They plan for the best and stack the odds in their favour. Winners ask a key question that helps them hold themselves in high esteem. They ask, "Why not me?" When they see something that they like, or someone doing something that they admire to be of value, they ask, "Why not me? Then their self-confidence kicks in and they remind themselves they can achieve what they want in life.

Winners hold themselves in high esteem by feeling and knowing that life wants them to succeed. Life wants them to do well and to make a contribution. And who knows—the contribution could change the world for the better!

Winners take responsibility. A common theme amongst winners is their choice (and it is a choice) to take full responsibility for everything that happens to them in their lives (good or bad). Accepting responsibility automatically puts us in a position of greater power. It's the power to make our lives go in the direction that we want.

Start early with your child by getting them out of the "Johnny made me do it" habit. Sounds funny but this is where blaming and shifting responsibility starts.

All these qualities and characteristics make up the winner's profile. You can pick any two successful well-rounded people and separate them by their differences. But as you sort through their personality traits, what you'll discover are the many similarities that they have. What you'll uncover is the winner's profile that makes for a common link among them.

I really do appreciate the time we have spent together and I thank you for reading this book! Please visit my website at: *www.cftacoffsharbour.com.au*

www.ingramcontent.com/pod-product-compliance
Lightning Source LLC
Chambersburg PA
CBHW051848040426
42447CB00006B/756